T0128038

My Almost Heart

WILLOW SE
AND
LINDSAY MCLEOD

BALBOA.
PRESS
A DIVISION OF HAY HOUSE

Balboa Press books may be ordered through booksellers or by contacting:

Balboa Press
A Division of Hay House
1663 Liberty Drive
Bloomington, IN 47403
www.balboapress.com.au
1 (877) 407-4847

Print information available on the last page.

ISBN: 978-1-5043-1365-0 (sc)
ISBN: 978-1-5043-1366-7 (e)

Balboa Press rev. date: 07/11/2018

Contents

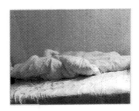

Nest

Will you heed your heartbeat's counsel
when it pleads unlock the gate
will you earth your feet in union
when they urge to relocate?
Will you stay safe, sound in shallows
or will you stroke out strong for depth
when banshee wailing selves
scream loud for sanctuary's breath,
can you eat your suite of blessings
and still sleep soft beneath her wings
and relish in deliciousness
that love brushed slumber brings.

Brewed

Excessive havoc in the detail
I consult the esoteric mouse
who obliterates my crystal dream
unblinds with disinfected douse,
smoothed the smorgasbord of Ley lines
that seethed seismic on my palm
I relinquished my delinquency
sailed in augurships of calm,
sidestepped the curlicues of snail shells
climbed in the teapot with the leaves
and steering with a golden earring
deciphered the unsyphoned, jumbled seas,
landing safe my copper coracle
I wrote the answer on the shore
'til the tide crept in and stole it
and left as many questions as before.

Flutter

A hope might fall both ways
if you forget to hold its hand
as it emerges from its chrysalis
all alone it cannot stand

wing clipped and willpower wavering
distant vision darkly dimmed
faltering on its flight path
flapping full against the wind

But when the chance presents
from our precious yesterskies
we might see beneath rough camouflage
strip away The World's disguise

and see all we have was ever there
just beyond our fingertips
reach out and touch our future's butterfly
as soft as lovers' lips.

Otherly

How the world hastens
to hush your heart
how it chastens the tender
for the magic they impart,
given freely to ghosts
that don't understand
can't capture the rapture
an eerie echo to aband.

Cold caste ears that hear no music
steel capped boots that feel no dance
with mawkish masked malevolence
in guise of normalcy to entrance,
who wear weak worths like bright medallions
expect us all to fall in line
yet heaven hewed us curious
from a dot to dot design.

Subterrain

As the light hit the pit of our cavern
prehistory daubed across its walls,
painted portents were ever our talismans
to forgive and forget and forestall.

Our fossils deposited with ancient odes
skeletal relics of all we once dreamed,
grounded powder memories time erodes
fall through the gap of what is and what seemed.

Buried rest havens for worn, weary souls
ribs that point fingers at God through the sod,
for poking the dreams that we wove full of holes
pushing us hard to life's edge with a prod.

We ponder the quandary of either side
watching the grains in the hourglass fall,
and hungry ghosts beckon to be our guides
but we avoid their gaze and their call.

...

We scramble through shambolic rubble
stand on the shoulders of all our mistakes,
and ease away all of our aching knots
take our hearts in our hands and remake.

Remoulding the folds and the creases
shaping a smoother revitalised form,
refashion our passionate portrait
burnishing all that we ever adored.

Hood

Should I pull this arrow from my chest
I do not know what's left or best,
afraid all this love might leak away
that was never there before today,

or perhaps carve out a hideaway hollow
where none can reach me, touch or follow,
safe and sound up in the branches
not daring now to take my chances,

whittling warily my bravado's bow
cloaked up close from one who knows,
or place my faith in those dear hands,
thus embrace a brand new ampersand.

Candyflossoms

And so, I'll stick my neck out
standing knee deep in this sea,
lift you high upon my shoulders
where we might see beyond
the crease,
inside cerise soaked sunsets
beckoning empyrean repose,
soft cradled, kissed in angel wisps
where our love making flows.

Real Ease

You tumbleweed my insides
spinning flinging at a pace
and undermine my cornerstone
let shuttered butterflies escape,
liberation sensation burst in multitude
cascading fresh tears of verisimilitude
that irrigate the barren ground
of haloed heart so long uncrowned,
untapped abundant effervescent springs
that sever soiled puppet strings,
enabling sweetened marionettes
to dance inside this untied breast
kick starting pulmonary pulses
with rhythmic ebbs of hopeful zest.

Orb

But tonight when we
send our hearts flying
out past the moon
with its lopsided grin
and whirling through
veils of diadem stars,
through puff tufts
of Nephelae kin.

Bellows

Soft sighs of senses
breathe in undulating waves,
soaked into skin and freeing
all our secret selves enslaved,
where once accursed chains
kept us enclosed in castle walls,
whilst shackled to our fears
to save a never ending fall.

Casting off the weighted cloak,
dusting off decrepit mantle
wings beat in new skies evoked
ricocheting off the anvil,
sparks set aflame to Phoenix's rise
detonating an explosive revival,
love that is seen as bright gems in our eyes
celebrating the diamond's arrival.

Heaven and Held

Entwined, blind in this circle of mercies,
become belovéd, emparadised,
star sequined cloaked and soaked in bliss,
become bedazzled, romanticised,

unfolded blanket of night wrapped about us,
the only light left pours out of our eyes,
silent voices decrypted from once before
cleansing dewdrop songs of soul's cries.

But when our hands reach out over the schism
made from all that has kept us apart,
dissolving aeons with blesséd reunion
as palms cradle, sheltering our hearts.

Pure if I

Our sequel swept up in the overflow
sweet memory romanced by the flavour,
the dregs washed away in our baptism
lucent infusing the goodness to savor,
the tip of my tongue on your next ladder rung
seen through the apple of evermore eyes,
sliding and gliding beyond the blue
past fluttering stuttering sighs,
on the wings of this rapturous remedy
plumes of hope that still live in these hearts,
a gentle felicitous flurry
purifying tendrils of tenderness paths,
that lead us once more to the ocean
where our chances kiss long on the shore
and limitless skies open up their arms
welcomes us back through a door to adore.

Blushus

Cracking solid ice of frozen fears
melting sullied snowflakes with my tears,
the final fleck that caused the avalanche
that had been building up for years.

Soaring, thawing out my maiden heart
caring bearskin wrapped around,
nestling, safeful feel of all that fur
warmth of brand new sunrise found,

and in the rosy glow of morning
whilst slumber softly slipped away,
you woke and smiled next to me
ensured tomorrows and today.

Revital

Salving seedlings of renewal
burst up through the nourished land
and rejuvenate my life force
osmotic waves push to expand

thrusting through eternal earth
reach for the sunshine's ever glow
purifying salted teardrops clean
transform my maybes into know

sweet watered with a rain dance
called from new clouds a chance today
and I will post the scarecrow of my past
to drive the doubts and ghosts away.

Floribunda

Tiptoeing cautious through the hopelands
squinting hard by candlelight
humming fireflies illuminate
to guide us through the night,
musk scented earth that grounds us
placing footprints in the real
and moonlight beacons brightly
upon our shimmering path revealed,
that leads us to a honeyed place
of jasmine infused perfection
where lightsome stars will all revere
our blesséd resurrection.

Angel

She wore the weight of the world on
her shoulders like a pair of angel's wings,
haloed her head with clouded thoughts
kicked gates shut t'were once opening,
but still she felt the echoes
in the chambers of her heart,
it sighed her name in heavenly hues
painting a finer celestial art
across her skin in silken spirals
that she remembered from his touch,
candlelit hush in quietude's quilt
shadow playing mimes of nonesuch,
the toss and turn in the dead of night
alternatives perched at the foot of her bed,
masqueraded Pucks playing frightful tricks
jostling with words heard in her head,
and so she spurs her Pegasus bareback
through skies that lead back to the start,
drops burdening worry weights earthbound
dispatching her doubts to the gods to depart,
and gallops back to love's hub in her memory
framed by a sun setting thresholded kiss,
unties the reins that restrain her
ruffles her feathers to fly into bliss.

Perchance

Beneath every confusing imperative
smiles the song of the coin in the flip
halt havering in illusionary idylls
dive deep into destiny's drip,
to float on a note in the miniature
kiss delicious, simplistic and whole
marvel in the shroud lifted vistas
dulcify the drift in the shift of our souls.

My Almost Heart

A thousand diaphanous dragonflies,
a million soft soulful sighs,
the military heart beats advance
and retreat in the Tango Criollo dance.

The partners fall prey to the rhythm,
light released from their pairing, a prism,
penetrates like fine lace, with a nebulous grace,
steps that lead to a chrysalis kingdom.

Where the fortress of mirroring shards
sentient sentinels wait en garde,
whilst the aromatic beseeching sea breeze
advances to tempt and to tease.

But stony battlements and glowering towers
have no power when love comes to flower,
no drawbridge, no sword, no armour, no pike
were ever defense against two hearts alike.

Dreamcatching

You might have known
what you could get
when you try to catch
clouds in a butterfly net,
you might have known
what you might feel
when you hoist in
the sun with your fishing reel
but all of the other
is never to try
and be left ever after
only wondering why.

Skylight

Your voice that night ate whole my darkness,
relit candles recessed inside of me,
devouring the scowling demons to dust,
re-igniting youthful incendiary.
As we climbed up love's hill draped in nightness,
fireworks blossoming brilliant 'tween stars,
enveloping arms embraced tight in their glory,
offering galaxies on the path that is ours.

Dancing like light around bright constellations
holding the Fate of our hearts in our hands,
two spellbound dervishes spinning,
inhabiting ambrosian lands.
I was summoned so strong by the angel's song
all those parts of me long lost were found,
when my head and my heart flew to heaven
and drew my love from the earth new, unbound.

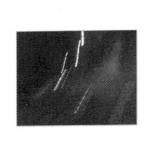

Peregrination

This shaft from your heart tore my aegis apart,
hurled me far from my Faraday cage,
dragged me into the light for the title fight,
transformed the understudy waiting backstage,
escaping from shadowing puppetry,
splitting cords of masterful grip,
the spotlight, empty, was expecting you,
Sherpa, to guide my metamorphosis trip.

Noir Abattoir

From this we are assembled
a sordid scar tissue mosaic
from all our stars that trembled
close clipped hearts awash with ache,

we bevelled dishevelled demons
sculpted into a formational frieze
hem all the nerve endings fraying
strap sutures stem all our dis-ease,

but we keep picking at our stitches
put our foot down, gather speed
mark ministrations of momentum
as we stampede toward the bleed

garotting sharply the carotid
saves the noose from burning rope
yet our spectres haunt our defectors
who ring a rosy play with hope.

Lupine

Hunkered low down on my haunches
quiet hiding from light shines of moon,
nightshade my deadlier dwelling
protection from my reflected cocoon,

my ringing symmetry of invisibility
kept me safe, all unseen, all unheld,
'til the daughter of dawn took her knife to my night
and all the darkness inside me expelled,

leaping out from cold faith of thorns,
I rose ribbon scarred but resolute,
stirred in my heart by a drum beat march,
looked straight at the sun to salute,

shaking hands with my impolite shadow,
she whispered low I should never look back
to a past that's yet haunted by howling
like a wolf pack heart attack.

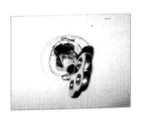

Turning

Cogged thoughts slam jammed,
riveted to the master plan
slashing differential lines
across the soothsayer's hands,

knifed networks of engravéd slaves,
chained to the remains of spectres,
rejecting all those lessons learned
and forgetting all the lectures.

Kowtowing in abject disgrace
prostrating soul to the filthy Fates
watching the gears turning slowly
as the machine reanimates,

reactivating pipe dream motion
that clicks to the tick of today,
another page torn from the calendar
as the future has its way.

Cord

With a suitcase full of dreams
and bursting pocketfuls of hope
we will climb once more to Heaven
upon that rainbowed arc of rope,

dust off all of the cowebbed clouds
scrub brilliant blue the mottled skies
and accept the blessings dressing us
without whats, whens, wheres or whys,

cast away the doubting harness
fling away the past times quilt
stand, panning in this riverbed
sort out the gold dust from the silt,

amity accord that forms a silken string
links us tight to our gossamer wings,
we vault free from a fault in the altar stone
taste love's kiss above all other things.

Ambrosia

Dew dropped drenched and dripping
honey healed in blossom's balm
climbing slowly out of amber
into summer's open arms,

fragranced fealty of our flora
bespangled our bowers of belief
beside a tear of awful autumn
fallen like the first forgetful leaf,

crouching close eternal embers
warming our hearts from wintry winds
but love's seedling still remembers
sends forth new shoots from season's sin.

Lunascene

Tonight our hearts swing in the hammock
held by our hopes from the horns of the moon
and sing out to the star studded indigo
for stellar sign to decipher our swoon
and as we search all the heavens for answers
'mong falling stars, we both wisp the same prayer,
that the world will tip its hat to the gods
for a flourishing fate we can share.

Sash

We'll keep our clouds all silver lined up
we'll keep our hopes all close at hand
and clamber up life's jagged edges
flying in tomorrow's Neverland,
where Paradise has ever beckoned since
we tasted of the ripened fruit
steering clear of pessimism's poison
a quicksilver serum that pollutes.
We'll dance to destiny's drumbeat
scattering flowers at our feet
become entwined about the Maypole
worship at the shrine of all that's sweet.

Ballast

Who dares to sit there unafraid
upon the threshold of the heart
who'll carry me over the brink
compelling dreaded fears to part
because I trusted in safe hands before
to release my rusted locks
that led me up the garden path
to a frustration of rocks.
So I'll sail solo on the open blue
battle the chattel in my hold
'til the wind whips it clear from my eyeline
and the last shed of tears is dissolved.

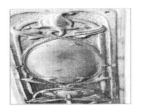

Enchase

All our dusty unjustified biases
all the ways that we choose to mistrust,
all the ways we refuse to surrender
our old armour ablister with rust,

fears yield behind shielding
tremors within the tin coat,
tears fall out of sharp corners
filling up our fortresses' moat,

the gift of the gauntlet a challenge
a hand that once fit like a glove,
a gold ring that leaves brand new marks of its own
erasing the engravings of love.

Harborage

Jump thumping heart stomps
back cracking flashes of fire
while I wrestle for balance
upon the chasm's high wire,
teetering to cheat the detractors
trembling in their war crying winds
completely unbalanced because of the loss,
the absence of my Siamese twin,

slipping in the whip, hung by a hair
that's tied to a hope-roped winch
loosen the hold of the hand all too tight
whose fingers had started to pinch,
reveling in unloved garnered palms
and the clandestined clasp of restraint,
discovering at once that the hand that held mine
'neath the callous was soft as a saint's.

Unbuttoned

Embedded threads weave our woes
that hold together patchwork prisons
a heart shaped bulge in Ouroboros
who swallowed whole our crimson collision,

baubled, fancied and velvetted swathes
that drapes capes over our shying shames
that cannot be faced in a lighted place
without reordering the rainbow of blame,

sweeping up the ragged remnants
refashioning a doublet a la mode
searching for sunrise 'cross rooftops
where of late our tragedy crowed.

Consumed

Butter candied and sugar dripped promises
tightly packaged in cellophane words,
cracked and attacked the sweetness attracts
from the shadows dark scavenging birds,
but the bitter and sour centres sicken
the syrup sticking to forgeries foils
as slowly the slithering serpent awakes
shedding scales as the future uncoils,
life laps with an untwisted tongue
ingesting a jolt vaulting start
equilibrium lurches from all love has purchased
and leaks through a moth eaten heart.

Harmonium

Fireworks hit and splinter the sky,
cracking cornices off the moon,
we collect our scattered notes of hope,
propose, compose a sweeter tune,
as bundles of stardust topple down
glitterfall balming crochetted chords,
reaching again for the song we once knew
underscored lyrics of love our reward.

Precipice

Love might be blind but
it feels and it sniffs
when it ventures too close
to suspicion's cliffs,

to stumble in a bundle
with our caution tightly wrapped
is an unparachuted folly
with fears forever trapped,

the freefall from forever
pulling feverishly on the cord
balancing out terminal velocity
upon the dead end of the sword.

Encore

The hiss of the wide open high hat
our reformation in the rain
drowned in the tears of the nightingale's song
we swim to the surface again,

absorbed in love soaked undulation
salt cleansed pores of purification,
renewed and imbued with lungfuls of lyrics
upon the waves of our standing ovation.

P.S.

We symbiotically surrendered
to the postscript in surprise
waving our white flags
released resistance to the skies,
stretched out our broken arms
across the Mariana Trench
we built our arch of amity
waltzed away our dour defence.

No more comfort sitting high astride
the backward flying blackbird
no metered masks suspending breath
or ventriloquist vocals heard,
with stronger hearts and softer eyes
thus we will tend each other's wounds
recalibrate our Terra Firma and
marching onward newly groomed.

Uncollared, Uncuffed

Jumbled in the wash I quash
wet humbled sullied sobbing
unlaundered on this carousel
soft circus music throbbing,
I dried the damp in air-spin
pegged small wonders on the line
and watched them dance miraculous
reach past their trapeze for the sky.

Letters Prey

Lazy circles were sculpted by vultures
upon a path that was sprinkled with tears
who salaciously devoured the droplets
sucking the life out of all we revere,
pick at the carcass of all our lost promises
worry the wound that's still new at our breast
we scavenge our ravishing remnants
scatter the brood at our shrieking behest.

Our hands grasping fistfuls of power
we peeled back the skin of the sky
stamp our feet at the vampire's departure
take careful aim as the archer lets fly,
it shoots toward moon beaming miracles
downpours a glittering, flickering cascade
that strips off our masquerade blinding
sets us free from life's bourgeois charade.

Belle

I tasted love's unsifted naiveté
like powdered sugar 'pon my tongue
lapped at the wish kissing flavours
'tween lips where my hungerness clung,
when the caress of blessing fingers
traced sacred scripture across my skin
our aching arches made altars
souls singing from our angels within,
that lift us to world's undiscovered
to a heaven that is better than real
cocooned with stars to the tune of the moon
sighing cries to love's carillon peal.

Glissade

That double spiral starcase
our sudden sensual ascent
we spring with wing-tipped wishing
enticing spice all heaven sent,
lost and found inside each other
perfectly balanced on the rim
afloat in balm two tender lovers
dulcifying demons from within,
sweet siren song entreating us
taste of love we've never known
we make a snowflake palace
around our numinous crystal throne,
lit by the sparks of souls electric
bathe in the oceans of our eyes
we ponder at the wondrousness
of cosmic cognizance descried,
lifted high on heaven's pointes
and swept into bright paradise
we spring arabesque in loving quest
to face our embraces with emprise.

Untressed

When we plaited ribbons of safety
into each other's knotted dread
teased our platitudes of gratitude
untied the tyrant's gnarling thread,
removed locks of bejewelled cruelty
shrugged off the silver draping chains
tugged loose tenderness' tendrils
setting free our unmanicured pains,
let them drown in deep seas of tranquility
robbed of breath and at last put to rest
let us rise through the flickering half light
back to the gleam of sweet sunlight undressed.

Mistral

Our heart's shrinking ransom
hung up high on harpoons,
vying for flying handsome
in a love puffed air balloon,
flung free of false directions
by The World's four winds at war
in sight of all we once aspired to
flipping fast within the draw,
to finally touch the phosphorescence
like promised comets in our sky
we kiss each other's wingtips
singing sweet mulled lullabies.

Touch

Discarding delinquent daisy chains
a coast of desires all lazy with blame,
delirious in denial's dial smiling
intoxicated by evocative claims,

strong hands that are gentled by nightfall
reach out for her there where she sighs,
'neath wysteria's showerful bowers
the wait sated in limned lover's cries,

her moan of his name in the darkness
casts a spell, a devouring dawn,
she rises to meet his beseeching call
entranced by its entreating denouement.

Truth

Ink dried and winked
at Veritas lying bare,
her tattoos of hypocrisy
shed in silken disrepair,

foiled by gargoyled profiles,
by unshaved, mephitic shames,
she purified her razor's blade
in heart's coruscating flames,

sliced at her quill willing it
to spill a neoteric epic tale,
dipping her pen in the wishing well
of love's battered holy grail,

reading her conscience still close unclipped
kept safe from the wastrel's weak wail,
then gripping the tip of the wish to her lips
she kisses past promises to prevail.

Drift

But we parachuted down
from our bridge of birds
to an earth feather dusted
by fur flying words.

Sweeping up forgotten flotsam
dissolving jaundiced jetsam,
falling back into each other
that was ever our protection.

Moulding a nest from molten stars
and woven from willow's boughs,
improving petalled promises
and honouring sacred vows.

We flew to the rise of dawning
quenched afloat in delirium's bath
at last at rest in heaven's breast
to follow tomorrow's path.

Paged

Slumber sings its lilting lullaby
drifting us to dreamy realms
as the scroll falls from our fingers
imprinted stories overwhelmed
where curing cloudbursts cry
for sorrow lost in the deluge
until the words wash off the paper
and shape a place for me and you.

Highness

Embracing unarmed Armageddon
wearing but this woven crown of scorn
I learned to reach into the mirror
remove that garland, be reborn,

casting out the tawdry heirlooms
washing leaden memories away
smoothing off the jagged crystal
dust off my tattered wrap of disarray,

standing tall in the halls of ancestry
burning caskets from the cellars below
hoisting flags festooned with finery
striding strong 'til the drawbridge is low,

to meet the seething mass anarchic
that sieges just beyond the gates
with my battered sword and crooked faith
prepared to face whate'er awaits,

standing fierce and tall unwavering
legs spread, strong hands on hips,
I will motion the gods 'en garde'
and every doubt will be eclipsed,

...

and I will see expressions altered
see demon's ragged smiles erased
when they realise I'm cast stronger
without the weight of armour plates,

that I will tolerate no longer or bow
'neath scant mercies of the Fates,
that I will champion my own life
and conquer all they obfuscate.

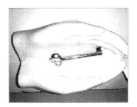

The Key

Soothed loose of the Houdini handcuffs
we climb again for the sky giant's glow
kissing the wrist of heart's industry
sorely missed in our recent ago,

we've sealed our sorrows in Pandora's boxes
placed forgiveness in forever's firm hands
eased away doubts, brow furrows smoothed out
blowing breath on bright embers to fan,

from cooling spark to a proud conflagration
there supernatural examples were formed,
all the lessons imparted embrightened us to
embrace the bonfire of love and be warmed.

Sliver

All the lessons inscribed on my skeleton
shuddering sighs from perpetual lips
all those soft centred linings in cumulus cries
brought my compromise into eclipse

the rain embossed lost on my hope chest
tore my parasols of protection away
then bare I declared it a stale mate
lacing boots round my cold feet of clay

thus I climbed on my red velvet rocking horse
dug in my heels and I let my mare run
back where nothing could find me behind me
to my home through a crack in the sun.

Shhh

When I felt forever's fingertips
pressing soft against my lips
and present's clawing bleat
gnawing raw at my feet
this push me-pull you heart of mine
casts blind around for hopeful sign
then a whisper kisses 'listen'
kisses listen... kisses listen.

About the Authors

Willow Se

Willow, a Celt, hears the zephyrs call of her mothers before to find a voice for her soul. She is a published children's author, prize winner for prose and lead vocalist with FFashionablyLate (SA). Romadic of many lands, the Fates decreed she wash up on Lindsay's horizon. Their co-creating induced ***My Almost Heart*** and a metaphysical metamorphosis

Lindsay McLeod

Lindsay trips over the horizon every morning. He has won several awards for poetry and short fiction and co-authored ***My Almost Heart*** with fellow poet Willow and boasts 50 poetry publications. He currently writes on the sandy southern edge of the world, where

the sea and the sky wrestle for supremacy at his letterbox. He prefers to support the underdog. It is presently an each-way bet.

Printed in the United States
By Bookmasters